What on Earth . . . ?

by the same author

MAGIC MIRROR
and other poems for children

MIDNIGHT FOREST
and other poems

edited by Judith Nicholls
WORDSPELLS

POPCORN PIE
(Mary Glasgow Publications)

WHAT ON EARTH...?

*Poems with a
Conservation Theme*

*Edited by
Judith Nicholls
Illustrated by
Alan Baker*

faber and faber
LONDON · BOSTON

First published in 1989
by Faber and Faber Limited
3 Queen Square London WC1N 3AU
Reprinted in 1990 and 1991

Photoset by Parker Typesetting Service Leicester
Printed in England by Clays Ltd, St Ives plc

A CIP record for this book is available
from the British Library

ISBN 0 571 15262 7

For Guy and Debbie,
with love

Contents

Introduction

The world of dew is
A world of dew . . . and yet,
And yet . . .

Kobayashi Issa (1763–1827)

How we value and care for our natural resources is a topical issue and becomes more so as we approach the end of the second millennium. Organizations concerned with conservation increase, television documentaries become more frequent, recycled paper has reached the small provincial high street. Each year more and more information books appear on library and retail shelves giving us the latest, shocking facts about acid rain, squandered energy, pesticide overkill, nuclear waste and disappearing countryside.

What of the poets? Have they been content to sit in splendid isolation in their ivory towers, quietly contemplating stars and the meaning of life – or have they, too, been concerned with the potential erosion of many of our invaluable resources? And just how new *is* the cry for conservation?

This anthology sets out to provide a selection of poets' responses to these two questions. It does not attempt to cover every issue; inevitably there will be passionate devotees of some specialist interests who will discover gaps. It has largely avoided the issue of war and its devastating effects on the environment on the grounds that there are already good war anthologies available. It does attempt to avoid the trap of offering a large number of 'protest poems' which are more protest than poetry!

While the poems can, of course, be read individually, at random, considerable thought has gone into the overall sequence. The book begins at a gentle pace with a newly created earth, leads eventually to the brink of destruction and ends on a note of hope for the future.

What on Earth . . .? will be of interest to teachers and pupils approaching a conservation topic and looking for something to develop the largely factual ideas of the new reference books in this area. It will offer a starting point to encourage pupils to express in discussion or in writing their own feelings about any of these important issues. It is hoped that it will also be of interest to many general readers concerned with *What on Earth . . .* we have done, are doing and will do in the future to our long-suffering planet.

Judith Nicholls
December 1988

This Newly Created World

Pleasant it looked,
this newly created world.
Along the entire length and breadth
of the earth, our grandmother,
extended the green reflection
of her covering
and the escaping odors
were pleasant to inhale.

Anon, Winnebago Indian

'Pleasure it is'

Pleasure it is
To here, iwis,
The birds sing;
The dere in the dale,
The shepe in the vale,
The corne springing.
God's purveaunce
For sustenaunce
It is for man:
Then we always
To him give praise,
And thank him than,
And thank him than.

Attributed to William Cornish (early 16th century)

iwis: indeed
purveaunce: providence, provision

Tree

As a child
I looked to the sky
and saw
a riverweed frond
Silhouetted
Against the clouds

Rippling with the
Current of wind
It teased and beckoned
Climb up
On my shoulder
Called the tree

Clasped tight
To the giant's waist
I felt a rocking
Canopy above
Echo through age
Crinkled bark

Spiralling onwards
the slenderest bough
Boasted sights
and excitement
Worthy of heavy breath
and sweat

Crouched on a high
Wooden shoulder
I carved my name
Into the deep
Ochre skin
Deft and proud

I greened over
the raw wound
With a crumpled leaf
but the Tree
shivered
Blood ran sticky yellow
and I cried

Adam Stanley (aged 15)

Spring

Nothing is so beautiful as Spring –
  When weeds, in wheels, shoot long and lovely and lush;
  Thrush's eggs look little low heavens, and thrush
Through the echoing timber does so rinse and wring
The ear, it strikes like lightnings to hear him sing;
  The glassy peartree leaves and blooms, they brush
  The descending blue; that blue is all in a rush
With richness; the racing lambs too have fair their fling.

What is all this juice and all this joy?
  A strain of the earth's sweet being in the beginning
In Eden garden. – Have, get, before it cloy,
  Before it cloud, Christ, lord, and sour with sinning,
Innocent mind and Mayday in girl and boy,
  Most, O maid's child, thy choice and worthy the winning.

Gerard Manley Hopkins (1844–89)

Turtle

In this cool cave-eyrie
indistinguishable from the rock
I, turtle, have not blinked
while birds have wheeled, flown south,
a thousand times
– and my friend, the bristlecone,
has steered his oldest bough
into the setting sun
until it rests upon itself.

On the plains the people fidget.
They kiss, scratch and shout 'Yippee',
but they do not know the calmness
of foreheads lightly touching,
– damp sand.

Worlds full of fickle pictures of themselves,
they have so little underground.

Sometimes they make smoke-clouds,
rain grows small and spiteful,
black patches creep across the plains,
turn grey
– and my cataracts return,
my shell grows brittle,
the bristlecone shrugs,
curls against the wind.

If only they were quiet
they could feel the sun long before it rises.

When the glitter hurts my eyes
I sink into my shell
and watch, in its faint shadows,
giant lizards pick their nervous way
between the turtles sleeping on the shore.
They rest, in jungle-caves and ice-cliffs,
waiting to come back.

I, turtle, lay my neck
on roots of the bristlecone, my friend.

There is no hurry with this egg.

John Latham

'I shall vanish'

I shall vanish and be no more,
But the land over which I now roam
Shall remain
And change not.

Anon, Omaha Indian

Fairy Tale

He built himself a house,
     his foundations,
     his stones,
     his walls,
     his roof overhead,
     his chimney and smoke,
     his view from the window.

He made himself a garden,
     his fence,
     his thyme,
     his earthworm,
     his evening dew.

He cut out his bit of sky above.

And he wrapped the garden in the sky
and the house in the garden
and packed the lot in a handkerchief

and went off
lone as an arctic fox
through the cold
unending
rain
into the world.

Miroslav Holub
(translated from Czech by
George Theiner)

Composed upon Westminster Bridge, September 3, 1802

Earth has not anything to show more fair:
Dull would he be of soul who could pass by
A sight so touching in its majesty:
This City now doth, like a garment, wear
The beauty of the morning; silent, bare,
Ships, towers, domes, theatres, and temples lie
Open unto the fields, and to the sky;
All bright and glittering in the smokeless air.
Never did sun more beautifully steep
In his first splendour, valley, rock, or hill;
Ne'er saw I, never felt, a calm so deep!
The river glideth at his own sweet will:
Dear God! the very houses seem asleep;
And all that mighty heart is lying still!

William Wordsworth (1770–1850)

'Who builds?'

Who builds? Who builds? Alas, ye poor,
If London day by day 'improves',
Where shall ye find a friendly door
When every day a home removes?

Anon (mid-19th century)

Smoke-blackened Smiths

Swarte-smeked smethes, smatered with smoke,
Drive me to deth with den of here dintes:
Swich nois on nightes ne herd men never,
What knavene cry and clatering of knockes!
The cammede kongons cryen after 'Col! col!'
And blowen here bellewes that all here brain brestes.
'Huf, puf,' seith that on, 'Haf, paf,' that other.
They spitten and sprawlen and spellen many spelles,
They gnawen and gnacchen, they grones togidere,
And holden hem hote with here hard hamers.
Of a bole hide ben here barm-felles,
Here shankes ben shakeled for the fere-flunderes.
Hevy hameres they han that hard ben handled,
Stark strokes they striken on a steled stocke.
'Lus, bus, las, das,' rowten by rowe.
Swiche dolful a dreme the Devil it todrive!
The maister longeth a litil and lasheth a lesse,
Twineth hem twein and toucheth a treble.
'Tik, tak, hic, hac, tiket, taket, tik, tak,
Lus, bus, lus, das'. Swich lif they leden,
Alle clothemeres, Christ hem give sorwe!
May no man for brenwateres on night han his rest.

Anon (15th century)

Smoke-blackened smiths, begrimed with smoke, drive me to death with the din of their blows: such noise by night no man ever heard, what crying of workmen and clattering of blows! The snub-nosed (? crooked?) changelings cry out for, 'Coal! coal!' and blow their bellows fit to burst their brains. 'Huf, puf', says that one, and 'Haf, paf', the other. They spit and sprawl and tell many tales, they gnaw and gnash, they groan

The Hammers

Noise of hammers once I heard,
Many hammers, busy hammers,
Beating, shaping, night and day,
Shaping, beating dust and clay
To a palace; saw it reared;
Saw the hammers laid away.

And I listened, and I heard
Hammers beating, night and day,
In the palace newly reared,
Beating it to dust and clay:
Other hammers, muffled hammers,
Silent hammers of decay.

Ralph Hodgson

together, and keep themselves hot with their hard hammers. Of a bull's hide are their
leather aprons, their legs are protected against the fiery sparks. Heavy hammers they
have that are handled hard, strong blows they strike on an anvil of steel. 'Lus, bus, las,
das', they crash in turn. May the Devil put an end to so miserable a racket. The
master-smith lengthens a little piece of iron, hammers a smaller piece, twists the two
together and strikes a treble note (?). Such a life they lead, all smiths who clothe horses
in iron armour, may Heaven punish them! For smiths who burn water (when they cool
hot iron in it) no man can sleep at night.

Trans. *R. T. Davies*

The Inheritor

I the sophisticated primate
Have stunted fingers on my feet,
And almost I control my climate,
And Everything is what I eat.

I wrote the story of Creation
When I discovered nudity:
The world is yours for exploitation.
I gave this charter unto me.

I traded in for my survival
My peaceful heart, my flealined coat;
Outpaced my vegetarian rival.
I have Creation by the throat.

Gerda Mayer

Noah and the Rabbit

'No land,' said Noah,
'There – is – not – any – land.
Oh, Rabbit, Rabbit, can't you understand?'

But Rabbit shook his head:
'Say it again,' he said;
'And slowly, please.
No good brown earth for burrows,
And no trees;
No wastes where vetch and rabbit-parsley grows,
No brakes, no bushes and no turnip rows,
No holt, no upland, meadowland or weald,
No tangled hedgerow and no playtime field?'

'No land at all – just water,' Noah replied,
And Rabbit sighed.
'For always, Noah?' he whispered, 'will there be
Nothing henceforth for ever but the sea?
Or will there come a day
When the green earth will call me back to play?'

Noah bowed his head:
'Some day . . . some day,' he said.

Hugh Chesterman

Countdown

Hurry, cried Progress,
and on to Earth
rushed

chain saw, axe and JCB,
crop sprays, oil slicks, pesticide;
battery farms and DDT,
smog and tear gas, monoxide.
Additives and sonic boom,
pills and parking lots,
concrete jungles, filled with gloom,
high-rise concrete flats.
Nuclear waste for just a taste
of what is still to come;
settle down, our shelter's warm –
do make yourself at home!
We've cigarettes to blacken lungs –
never mind the bill;
who needs seeds and forestry
with acid rain to kill?

Come in, come in! cried Progress,
Let's light these cloudy skies –
and crept towards the button,
rubbing smoke-filled eyes.

Welcome, daughters,
to your land —
this ark is yours and mine.
Do watch your step,
the trap is set —
we only wait for Time.

Come in, my sons,
do feel at home;
come in and share the mirth!
I've played my part —
you alone
can rescue planet Earth.

Judith Nicholls

'I robbed the Woods'

I robbed the Woods –
The trusting Woods.
The unsuspecting Trees
Brought out their Burs and mosses
My fantasy to please.
I scanned their trinkets curious –
I grasped – I bore away –
What will the solemn Hemlock –
What will the Oak tree say?

Emily Dickinson (1830–86)

Moss-gathering

To loosen with all ten fingers held wide and limber
And lift up a patch, dark-green, the kind for lining cemetery
    baskets,
Thick and cushiony, like an old-fashioned doormat,
The crumbling small hollow sticks on the underside mixed with
    roots,
And wintergreen berries and leaves still stuck to the top –
That was moss-gathering.
But something always went out of me when I dug loose those
    carpets
Of green, or plunged to my elbows in the spongy yellowish
    moss of the marshes:
And afterwards I always felt mean, jogging back over the
    logging road,
As if I had broken the natural order of things in that
    swampland;
Disturbed some rhythm, old and of vast importance,
By pulling off flesh from the living planet;
As if I had committed, against the whole scheme of life, a
    desecration.

Theodore Roethke (1906–63)

The Poplar Field

The poplars are fell'd, farewell to the shade
And the whispering sound of the cool colonnade;
The winds play no longer and sing in the leaves,
Nor Ouse on his bosom their image receives.

Twelve years have elapsed since I last took a view
Of my favourite field, and the bank where they grew.
And now in the grass behold they are laid,
And the tree is my seat that once lent me a shade.

The blackbird has fled to another retreat
Where the hazels afford him a screen from the heat;
And the scene where his melody charm'd me before
Resounds with his sweet-flowing ditty no more.

My fugitive years are all hasting away,
And I must ere long lie as lowly as they,
With a turf on my breast and a stone at my head,
Ere another such grove shall arise in its stead.

'Tis a sight to engage me, if anything can,
To muse on the perishing pleasures of man;
Short-lived as we are, our enjoyments, I see,
Have a still shorter date, and die sooner than we.

William Cowper (1731–1800)

Felling Trees

Stop! I cried to them,
    But the noise of their saws
Cut out my final plea.
    Everything is dying;
Dark sky where the flats will be.

    Adrian Youd (aged 12)

The Hen

In the waiting room of the railway,
Not built for it,
A hen
Walks up and down.
Where, where has the stationmaster gone?
Surely no one
Will harm this hen?
Let us hope not! Then,
Out loud, let us say:
Our sympathy goes out to it
Even here, where it's in the way!

    Christian Morgenstern (1871–1914)
        (translated from German by
    W. D. Snodgrass and Lore Segal)

Song of the Battery Hen

We can't grumble about accommodation:
we have a new concrete floor that's
always dry, four walls that are
painted white, and a sheet-iron roof
the rain drums on. A fan blows warm air
beneath our feet to disperse the smell
of chicken-shit and, on dull days,
fluorescent lighting sees us.

You can tell me: if you come by
the North door, I am in the twelfth pen
on the left-hand side of the third row
from the floor; and in that pen
I am usually the middle one of three.
But, even without directions, you'd
discover me. I have the same orange-
red comb, yellow beak and auburn
feathers, but as the door opens and you
hear above the electric fan a kind of
one-word wail, I am the one
who sounds loudest in my head.

Listen. Outside this house there's an
orchard with small moss-green apple
trees; beyond that, two fields of
cabbages; then, on the far side of
the road, a broiler house. Listen:
one cockerel grows out of there, as
tall and proud as the first hour of sun.
Sometimes I stop calling with the others
to listen, and wonder if he hears me.

The next time you come here, look for me.
Notice the way I sound inside my head.
God made us all quite differently,
and blessed us with this expensive home.

Edwin Brock

To Walk on Grass

I remember what it was
to walk on grass
I remember when they used to
count the years
and number them
one by one. One after the next
An interesting tale
but no one to tell it to

And words like *crowds*,
and *birds* and *life* I recall
they never used to frighten me.

If only there was someone
who could remind me
what colours were
If only I could tell them in return
what it was
to walk on grass.

Gordon Macintosh

Old Johnny Armstrong

Old Johnny Armstrong's eighty or more
And he humps like a question-mark
Over two gnarled sticks as he shuffles and picks
His slow way to Benwell Park.

He's lived in Benwell his whole life long
And remembers how street-lights came,
And how once on a time they laid a tram-line,
Then years later dug up the same!

Now he's got to take a lift to his flat,
Up where the tall winds blow
Round a Council Block that rears like a rock
From seas of swirled traffic below.

Old Johnny Armstrong lives out his life
In his cell on the seventeenth floor,
And it's seldom a neighbour will do him a favour
Or anyone knock at his door.

With his poor hands knotted with rheumatism
And his poor back doubled in pain,
Why, day after day, should he pick his slow way
To Benwell Park yet again? –

O the wind in park trees is the self-same wind
That first blew on a village child
When life freshly unfurled in a green, lost world
And his straight limbs ran wild.

Raymond Wilson

The Beck Insists

It's not nostalgia, I don't
Even want them to send
'The Whitehaven News' anymore,
And to set foot in the village
Is to be confused by petrol pumps
Where the smithy stood,
A loft and pigsty tarted up
As Beckside Cottage,
Unknown names on first prize tickets
Telling me that I've become
An off-comer at Ennerdale Show.

But here at home,
The beck insists on running
Through remembered alders,
A surging flow that laps the rock
Where a dipper beckons
With a white shirt bob,
Before he skims upstream
And leads me to the source.

Tom Rawling

'When I heard the learn'd astronomer'

When I heard the learn'd astronomer,
When the proofs, the figures, were ranged in columns before
    me,
When I was shown the charts and diagrams, to add, divide,
    and measure them,
When I sitting heard the astronomer where he lectured with
    much applause in the lecture-room,
How soon unaccountable I became tired and sick,
Till rising and gliding out I wander'd off by myself,
In the mystical moist night-air, and from time to time
Look'd up in perfect silence at the stars.

Walt Whitman (1819–92)

Back Yard, July Night

Firefly, airplane, satellite, star –
How I wonder which you are.

William Cole

Sonic Boom

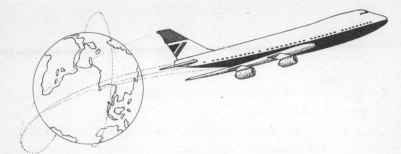

I'm sitting in the living room,
When, up above, the Thump of Doom
Resounds. Relax. It's sonic boom.

The ceiling shudders at the clap,
The mirrors tilt, the rafters snap,
And Baby wakens from his nap.

'Hush, babe. Some pilot we equip,
Giving the speed of sound the slip,
Has cracked the air like a penny whip.'

Our world is far from frightening; I
No longer strain to read the sky
Where moving fingers (jet planes) fly.
Our world seems much too tame to die.

And if it does, with one more *pop*,
I shan't look up to see it drop.

John Updike

5 Ways to Kill a Man

There are many cumbersome ways to kill a man:
you can make him carry a plank of wood
to the top of a hill and nail him to it. To do this
properly you require a crowd of people
wearing sandals, a cock that crows, a cloak
to dissect, a sponge, some vinegar and one
man to hammer the nails home.

Or you can take a length of steel,
shaped and chased in a traditional way,
and attempt to pierce the metal cage he wears.
But for this you need white horses,
English trees, men with bows and arrows,
at least two flags, a prince and a
castle to hold your banquet in.

Dispensing with nobility, you may, if the wind
allows, blow gas at him. But then you need
a mile of mud sliced through with ditches,
not to mention black boots, bomb craters,
more mud, a plague of rats, a dozen songs
and some round hats made of steel.

In an age of aeroplanes, you may fly
miles above your victim and dispose of him by
pressing one small switch. All you then
require is an ocean to separate you, two
systems of government, a nation's scientists,
several factories, a psychopath and
land that no one needs for several years.

These are, as I began, cumbersome ways
to kill a man. Simpler, direct, and much more neat
is to see that he is living somewhere in the middle
of the twentieth century, and leave him there.

Edwin Brock

Bang

When the goodies are all gone
what shall we do
with the old brown bag of an earth
but blow it up – BANG

Crumpled brown paper bag
scuttling along
the desolate white
lanes of the universe

Gerda Mayer

Benedic, anima mea

O Lord, how manifold are thy works! in wisdom hast thou made them all: the earth is full of thy riches.

from *Psalm 104, The Old Testament*

God's Grandeur

The world is charged with the grandeur of God.
  It will flame out, like shining from shook foil;
  It gathers to a greatness, like the ooze of oil
Crushed. Why do men then now not reck his rod?
Generations have trod, have trod, have trod;
  And all is seared with trade; bleared, smeared with toil;
  And wears man's smudge and shares man's smell: the soil
Is bare now, nor can foot feel, being shod.

And for all this, nature is never spent;
  There lives the dearest freshness deep down things;
And though the last lights off the black West went
  Oh, morning, at the brown brink eastward, springs –
Because the Holy Ghost over the bent
  World broods with warm breast and with ah! bright wings.

Gerard Manley Hopkins (1844–89)

In the Microscope

Here too are dreaming landscapes,
lunar, derelict.
Here too are the masses,
tillers of the soil.
And cells, fighters
who lay down their lives
for a song.

Here too are cemeteries,
fame and snow.
And I hear murmuring,
the revolt of immense estates.

Miroslav Holub
(translated from Czech by Ian Milner)

Wasp Nest

Be careful not to crush
This scalloped tenement:
Who knows what secrets
Winter has failed to find
Within its paper walls?

It is the universe
Looking entirely inwards,
A hanging lantern
Whose black light wriggles
Through innumerable chambers

Where hopes still sleep
In her furry pews,
The chewed dormitory
Of a forgotten tribe
That layered its wooden pearl.

It is a basket of memories,
A museum of dead work,
The spat Babel of summer
With a marvellous language
Of common endeavour.

Note: it is the fruit
Returning to the tree,
The world becoming a clock
For sleep, a matrix of pure
Energy, a book of many lives.

John Fuller

Minstrel's Song

There are, some people say, no riches in the bush.
But look at an ant hill:
It has a helmet providing shelter from the rain.
See that beetle:
His coat does not go round him
And yet it has three buttons.
A bird which lives there in the bush
Has a wooden house:
Who is the carpenter?
This bush cow wears boots
Like those of a soldier;
That baboon has a black coat
Like a policeman;
And the kingfisher has a silk gown.
Why, then, do some people say
There are no riches in the bush?

Anon (translated from Mende by K. L. Little)

from *Auguries of Innocence*

To see a World in a Grain of Sand
And a Heaven in a Wild Flower,
Hold Infinity in the palm of your hand
And Eternity in an hour.

A Robin Redbreast in a Cage
Puts all Heaven in a Rage.
A dove house fill'd with doves and pigeons
Shudders Hell thro' all its regions.
A dog starv'd at his Master's gate
Predicts the ruin of the State.
A Horse misus'd upon the Road
Calls to Heaven for Human blood.
Each outcry of the hunted Hare
A fibre from the Brain does tear.
A Skylark wounded in the wing,
A Cherubim does cease to sing.

William Blake (1757–1827)

Inversnaid

This darksome burn, horseback brown,
His rollrock highroad roaring down,
In coop and in comb the fleece of his foam
Flutes and low to the lake falls home.

A windpuff-bonnet of fawn-froth
Turns and twindles over the broth
Of a pool so pitchblack, fell-frowning,
It rounds and rounds Despair to drowning.

Degged with dew, dappled with dew
Are the groins of the braes that the brook treads through,
Wiry heathpacks, flitches of fern,
And the beadbonny ash that sits over the burn.

What would the world be, once bereft
Of wet and of wildness? Let them be left,
O let them be left, wildness and wet;
Long live the weeds and the wilderness yet.

Gerard Manley Hopkins (1844–89)

A Poem for the Rainforest

Song of the Xingu Indian

They have stolen my land;
the birds have flown,
my people gone.
My rainbow rises over sand;
my river falls on stone.

Amazonian Timbers, Inc.

This can go next –
here, let me draw the line.
That's roughly right,
give or take
a few square miles or so.
I'll list the ones we need.
No, burn the rest.
Only take the best,
we're not in this
for charity,
Replant? No –
you're new to this, I see!
There's plenty more
where that comes from,
no problem! Finish here –
and then move on.

Dusk

Butterfly, blinded
by smoke, drifts like torn paper
to the flames below.

Shadows

Spider,
last of her kind,
scuttles underground, safe;
prepares her nest for young ones. But
none come.

The Coming of Night

Sun sinks
behind the high canopy;
the iron men are silenced.

The moon rises,
the firefly wakes.
Death pauses for a night.

Song of the Forest

*Our land has gone,
our people flown.
Sun scorches our earth,
our river weeps.*

Judith Nicholls

In wildness is the preservation of the world.

Henry David Thoreau (1817–62)

Binsey Poplars
felled 1879

My aspens dear, whose airy cages quelled,
Quelled or quenched in leaves the leaping sun,
All felled, felled, are all felled;
   Of a fresh and following folded rank
       Not spared, not one
       That dandled a sandalled
     Shadow that swam or sank
On meadow and river and wind-wandering weed-
   winding bank.

O if we but knew what we do
     When we delve or hew –
Hack and rack the growing green!
     Since country is so tender
To touch, her being só slender,
That, like this sleek and seeing ball
But a prick will make no eye at all,
Where we, even where we mean

      To mend her we end her,
   When we hew or delve:
After-comers cannot guess the beauty been.
   Ten or twelve, only ten or twelve
     Strokes of havoc únselve
      The sweet especial scene,
   Rural scene, a rural scene,
   Sweet especial rural scene.

Gerard Manley Hopkins (1844–89)

Riddle

You could slake a small thirst
from my cup or take
my smooth worrybead
of a seed and cast up
slow centuries of growth. I'm planned
to outlast you, stand high
above you. Make me, raw stuff
for your saws, into stairs,
beams, doors, shelves, rough
firewood, fine chairs. I am air
for your breath, I am loam
for growth. You, who need Earth
for your home, must revere, must spare
me; there will be no birth,
only a dwindling to death without
me and my kind. We are beacons;
we flare to guide, to warn.
Watch our green burning; while we
live you come to no harm.

Pamela Gillilan

Gathering Leaves

Spades take up leaves
No better than spoons,
And bags full of leaves
Are light as balloons.

I make a great noise
Of rustling all day
Like rabbit and deer
Running away.

But the mountains I raise
Elude my embrace,
Flowing over my arms
And into my face.

I may load and unload
Again and again
Till I fill the whole shed,
And what have I then?

Next to nothing for weight;
And since they grew duller
From contact with earth,
Next to nothing for color.

Next to nothing for use.
But a crop is a crop,
And who's to say where
The harvest shall stop?

Robert Frost (1874–1963)

This Letter's to Say

Dear Sir or Madam,
This letter's to say
Your property
Stands bang in the way
Of Progress, and
Will be knocked down
On March the third
At half-past one.

There is no appeal,
Since the National Need
Depends on more
And still more Speed,
And this, in turn,
Dear Sir or Madam,
Depends on half England
Being tar-macadam.
(But your house will –
We are pleased to say –
Be the fastest lane
Of the Motorway).

Meanwhile the Borough
Corporation
Offer you new
Accommodation
Three miles away
On the thirteenth floor
(Flat Number Q
6824).

But please take note,
The Council regret:
No dog, cat, bird
Or other pet;
No noise permitted,
No singing in the bath
(For permits to drink
Or smoke or laugh
Apply on Form
Z 327);
No children admitted
Aged under eleven;
No hawkers, tramps
Or roof-top lunchers;
No opening doors
To Bible-punchers.

Failure to pay
Your rent, when due,
Will lead to our
Evicting you.
The Council demand
That you consent
To the terms above
When you pay your rent.

Meanwhile we hope
You will feel free
To consult us
Should there prove to be
The slightest case
Of difficulty.

With kind regards,
Yours faithfully . . .

Raymond Wilson

Windscale

The toadstool towers infest the shore:
Stink-horns that propagate and spore
    Wherever the wind blows.
Scafell looks down from the bracken band,
And sees hell in a grain of sand,
    And feels the canker itch between his toes.

This is a land where dirt is clean,
And poison pasture, quick and green,
    And storm sky, bright and bare;
Where sewers flow with milk, and meat
Is carved up for the fire to eat,
    And children suffocate in God's fresh air.

Norman Nicholson (1914–87)

from *The Deserted Village*

Sweet smiling village, loveliest of the lawn,
Thy sports are fled, and all thy charms withdrawn;
Amidst thy bowers the tyrant's hand is seen
And desolation saddens all thy green:
One only master grasps the whole domain,
And half a tillage stints thy smiling plain;
No more thy glassy brook reflects the day,
But choked with sedges, works its weedy way;
Among thy glades, a solitary guest,
The hollow sounding bittern guards its nest;
Amidst thy desert walks the lapwing flies,
And tires their echoes with unvaried cries.
Sunk are thy bowers, in shapeless ruin all,
And the long grass o'ertops the mouldering wall;
And trembling, shrinking from the spoiler's hand,
Far, far away thy children leave the land.
Ill fares the land, to hastening ills a prey,
Where wealth accumulates, and men decay:
Princes and lords may flourish, or may fade;
A breath can make them, as a breath has made;
But a bold peasantry, their country's pride,
When once destroyed, can never be supplied.

Oliver Goldsmith (1730–74)

from *Remembrances*

Summer's pleasures they are gone like to visions every one,
And the cloudy days of autumn and of winter cometh on.
I tried to call them back, but unbidden they are gone
Far away from heart and eye and for ever far away.
Dear heart, and can it be that such raptures meet decay?
I thought them all eternal when by Langley Bush I lay,
I thought them joys eternal when I used to shout and play
On its bank at 'clink and bandy', 'chock' and 'taw' and
  'ducking-stone',
Where silence sitteth now on the wild heath as her own
Like a ruin of the past all alone.

When I used to lie and sing by old Eastwell's boiling spring,
When I used to tie the willow boughs together for a swing,
And fish with crooked pins and thread and never catch a thing,
With heart just like a feather, now as heavy as a stone;
When beneath old Lea Close Oak I the bottom branches broke
To make our harvest cart like so many working folk,
And then to cut a straw at the brook to have a soak.
Oh, I never dreamed of parting or that trouble had a sting,
Or that pleasures like a flock of birds would ever take to wing,
Leaving nothing but a little naked spring.

Here was commons for their hills, where they seek for freedom
    still,
Though every common's gone and though traps are set to kill
The little homeless miners – oh, it turns my bosom chill
When I think of old Sneap Green, Puddock's Nook and Hilly
    Snow,
Where bramble bushes grew and the daisy gemmed in dew
And the hills of silken grass like to cushions to the view,
Where we threw the pismire crumbs when we'd nothing else to do,
All levelled like a desert by the never-weary plough,
All vanish'd like the sun where that cloud is passing now
And settled here for ever on its brow.

Oh, I never thought that joys would run away from boys,
Or that boys would change their minds and forsake such
    summer joys;
But alack, I never dreamed that the world had other toys
To petrify first feeling like the fable into stone,
Till I found the pleasure past and a winter come at last,
Then the fields were sudden bare and the sky got overcast,
And boyhood's pleasing haunts, like a blossom in the blast,
Was shrivelled to a withered weed and trampled down and
    done,
Till vanished was the morning spring and set the summer sun,
And winter fought her battle strife and won.

By Langley Bush I roam, but the bush hath left its hill,
On Cowper Green I stray, 'tis a desert strange and chill,
And the spreading Lea Close Oak, ere decay had penned its
    will,
To the axe of the spoiler and self-interest fell a prey,
And Crossberry Way and old Round Oak's narrow lane
With its hollow trees like pulpits I shall never see again,
Enclosure like a Buonaparte let not a thing remain,
It levelled every bush and tree and levelled every hill
And hung the moles for traitors – though the brook is running
    still
It runs a naked stream, cold and chill.

Oh, had I known as then joy had left the paths of men,
I had watched her night and day, be sure, and never slept
    agen,
And when she turned to go, oh, I'd caught her mantle then,
And wooed her like a lover by my lonely side to stay;
Ay, knelt and worshipped on, as love in beauty's bower,
And clung upon her smiles as a bee upon a flower,
And gave her heart my posies, all cropt in a sunny hour,
As keepsakes and pledges all to never fade away;
But love never heeded to treasure up the may,
So it went the common road to decay.

John Clare (1793–1864)

'We are going to see the rabbit . . .'

We are going to see the rabbit,
We are going to see the rabbit.
Which rabbit, people say?
Which rabbit, ask the children?
Which rabbit?
The only rabbit,
The only rabbit in England,
Sitting behind a barbed-wire fence
Under the floodlights, neon lights,
Sodium lights,
Nibbling grass
On the only patch of grass
In England, in England
(Except the grass by the hoardings
Which doesn't count.)
We are going to see the rabbit
And we must be there on time.

First we shall go by escalator,
Then we shall go by underground,
And then we shall go by motorway
And then by helicopterway,
And the last ten yards we shall have to go
On foot.

And now we are going
All the way to see the rabbit,
We are nearly there,
We are longing to see it,
And so is the crowd
Which is here in thousands
With mounted policemen
And big loudspeakers
And bands and banners,
And everyone has come a long way.
But soon we shall see it
Sitting and nibbling
The blades of grass
On the only patch of grass
In – but something has gone wrong!
Why is everyone so angry,
Why is everyone jostling
And slanging and complaining?

The rabbit has gone,
Yes, the rabbit has gone.
He has actually burrowed down into the earth
And made himself a warren, under the earth,
Despite all these people.
And what shall we do?
What *can* we do?

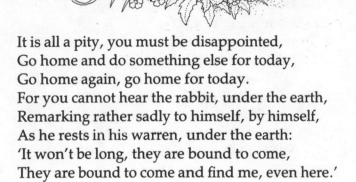

It is all a pity, you must be disappointed,
Go home and do something else for today,
Go home again, go home for today.
For you cannot hear the rabbit, under the earth,
Remarking rather sadly to himself, by himself,
As he rests in his warren, under the earth:
'It won't be long, they are bound to come,
They are bound to come and find me, even here.'

Alan Brownjohn

The Last Human

The animals are excited,
Their hearts are full of glee,
They're going to see the human,
The last in history.

But when they reach the zoo,
Their hearts fall with a flop.
He's not at all what they expected.
They cry, 'He's not much cop!'

'He does not jump or spring
Or pull a funny face.
He just sits there sadly –
He really is a case!'

'We want our money back,' they say,
'And want it back right now!
He hasn't got much bounce
And he hasn't got much pow!'

'Well, what do you expect?'
Is the answer that they hear.
'He's only got himself
And no one he holds dear.'

'How sad,' reply the animals.
'You'd better let him go,
He's far too unhappy
To keep him there on show.'

Louisa-Jane Snook (aged 14)

'This then is life'

This then is life,
Here is what has come to the surface after so many
   throes and convulsions.

How curious! how real!
Underfoot the divine soil, overhead the sun.

Walt Whitman (1819–92)

Sap-Whistle

Smooth-skinned sap-flooded
Hedgerow sycamore was best,
Bigger boys showed that
And where to make a half-moon notch,
How to circle-cut the bark,
Soothe with spit the knock
The repeated knock
Of the back of the knife,
But it was Grandmother's spell,
As if she held a willow wand,
Her doggerel, 'Willy willy wap,
Tip tip tap, take off your black cap',
That compelled the bark
To slide complete,
White thigh revealed.

The rest was paring, trial, craft,
Hollowing an inner space;
Wood wetted in the mouth
To ease the tube in place,
Exact match of nick and notch.
Then a young note piped
From her old breath.

Each year still when red wrinkles
Swell to burst the buds,
When young sap floods I make a whistle
Taste the maple, speak her spell.
I would hand it on but my grandson plays
Half a century from my hedgerow.

Tom Rawling

The Combe

The Combe was ever dark, ancient and dark.
Its mouth is stopped with bramble, thorn, and briar;
And no one scrambles over the sliding chalk
By beech and yew and perishing juniper
Down the half precipices of its sides, with roots
And rabbit holes for steps. The sun of Winter,
The moon of Summer, and all the singing birds
Except the missel-thrush that loves juniper,
Are quite shut out. But far more ancient and dark
The Combe looks since they killed the badger there,
Dug him out and gave him to the hounds,
That most ancient Briton of English beasts.

Edward Thomas (1878–1917)

'I lost a World'

I lost a World – the other day!
Has Anybody found?
You'll know it by the Row of Stars
Around its forehead bound.

A Rich man – might not notice it –
Yet – to my frugal Eye,
Of more Esteem than Ducats –
Oh find it – Sir – for me!

Emily Dickinson (1830–86)

'The shark is killed for its fin'

The shark is killed for its fin
The rhino is killed for its horn
The tiger is killed for its skin
What price the unicorn?

Anon

The Hope of Wings

The girl forces the gull's beak open with
A spoon and starts to scrape the oil away.
Rampant the sky's colours, legend and myth
Sustain the attention of those beset by
Traditional hungers, but now I foresee
A bird-emptied sky, the world's shores
Hilled with crippled things, the thick, black
Smothering oil murdering the hope of wings,
And this girl – she can't be into her teens –
Would, if her working now is a guide,
Spend all her years remaking these stunned birds
Littering the sea, dead flops among stones.
She'd give a white-winged creature to the sky
Before black tides destroy mere human words.

Brendan Kennelly

'He who binds'

He who binds to himself a joy
Does the winged life destroy;
But he who kisses the joy as it flies
Lives in eternity's sun rise.

William Blake (1757–1827)

Going, Going

I thought it would last my time –
The sense that, beyond the town,
There would always be fields and farms,
Where the village louts could climb
Such trees as were not cut down;
I knew there'd be false alarms

In the papers about old streets
And split-level shopping, but some
Have always been left so far;
And when the old part retreats
As the bleak high-risers come
We can always escape in the car.

Things are tougher than we are, just
As earth will always respond
However we mess it about;
Chuck filth in the sea, if you must:
The tides will be clean beyond.
– But what do I feel now? Doubt?

Or age, simply? The crowd
Is young in the M1 café;
Their kids are screaming for more –
More houses, more parking allowed,
More caravan sites, more pay.
On the Business Page, a score

Of spectacled grins approve
Some takeover bid that entails
Five per cent profit (and ten
Per cent more in the estuaries): move
Your works to the unspoilt dales
(Grey area grants)! And when

You try to get near the sea
In summer . . .
                              It seems, just now,
To be happening so very fast;
Despite all the land left free
For the first time I feel somehow
That it isn't going to last,

That before I snuff it, the whole
Boiling will be bricked in
Except for the tourist parts –
First slum of Europe: a role
It won't be so hard to win,
With a cast of crooks and tarts.

And that will be England gone,
The shadows, the meadows, the lanes,
The guildhalls, the carved choirs.
There'll be books; it will linger on
In galleries; but all that remains
For us will be concrete and tyres.

Most things are never meant.
This won't be, most likely: but greeds
And garbage are too thick-strewn
To be swept up now, or invent
Excuses that make them all needs.
I just think it will happen, soon.

Philip Larkin (1922–85)

The Flower-Fed Buffaloes

The flower-fed buffaloes of the spring
In the days of long ago,
Ranged where the locomotives sing
And the prairie flowers lie low:–
The tossing, blooming, perfumed grass
Is swept away by the wheat,
Wheels and wheels and wheels spin by
In the spring that still is sweet.
But the flower-fed buffaloes of the spring
Left us, long ago.
They gore no more, they bellow no more,
They trundle around the hills no more:–
With the Blackfeet, lying low,
With the Pawnees, lying low,
Lying low.

Vachel Lindsay (1879–1931)

The Day the Bulldozers Came

The day the bulldozers came
Rooks were building
Crazy egg baskets in the oaks;
Green flies sizzled by the pond
And a cold-eyed toad
Waited for them:

The day the bulldozers came
Squirrels were scattering
Up tree trunks,
And leapt from branches
That were hardly there.

The fox
Stirred in his sleep
As the ground trembled.
   'Ha ha!' he thought,
   'I'm quite safe,
Deep down in the Earth,
No one can get me here.'

Then the bulldozers came.

David Orme

Graveyard Scene

There are no names on the gravestones now,
They've been washed away by the rain.
The graveyard trees are skeletons now,
They will never wear leaves again.

Instead of a forest, the tower surveys
A bleak and desolate plain.
Those are not tears in the gargoyle's eyes,
They are droplets of acid rain.

John Foster

Poisoned Talk

Who killed cock robin?
I, said the worm,
I did him great harm.
He died on the branch of a withered tree
From the acid soil that poisoned me.

Who killed the heron?
I, mouthed the fish,
With my tainted flesh
I killed tern, duck and drake,
All the birds of the lake.

Who killed the lake?
I, boasted Industry,
I poisoned with mercury
Fish, plant and weed
To pamper men's greed.

Who killed the flowers?
I, moaned the wind,
I prowl unconfined,
Blowing acid rain
Over field, flood and fen.

Who killed the forest?
I ensured that it died,
Said sulphur dioxide,
And all life within it,
From earthworm to linnet.

Raymond Wilson

Owl

How mournfully the owl hoots
And who can tell what it denotes:
Across the dusk he sounds to me
Like the last owl on the last tree.

Gerda Mayer

'What cuckoos we are'

What cuckoos we are
If dense, without care,
Not knowing that nature knows best
We seek to heave
This miracled world
From its old and well-wrought nest.

John Kitching

Leviathan

You can't make whales
Make whales.
Hens don't seem to mind
Laying eggs for you.
The patient cow
Conceives at the squirt of a syringe.
Shoals of fry
Will populate concrete ponds,
But whales cannot be handled
Contained
Farmed
Made familiar like dolphins or lions
Herded like pigs or sheep.
Their procreation is their own affair
Their milk for their own young.
In death only does man
Find them valuable.

When none are left
Their monumental bones
Will stand stripped in museums,
Their pictures wonderful on the page
At W in a child's alphabet,
Like D for Dodo,
H for humanity.

Pamela Gillilan

Fishing

Fishing, if I, a fisher, may protest,
Of pleasures is the sweetest, of sports the best,
Of exercises the most excellent;
Of recreations the most innocent;
But now the sport is marred, and wott ye why?
Fishes decrease, and fishers multiply.

Thomas Bastard (1566–1618)

Take One Home for the Kiddies

On shallow straw, in shadeless glass,
Huddled by empty bowls, they sleep:
No dark, no dam, no earth, no grass –
Mam, get us one of them to keep.

Living toys are something novel,
But it soon wears off somehow.
Fetch the shoebox, fetch the shovel –
Mam, we're playing funerals now.

Philip Larkin (1922–85)

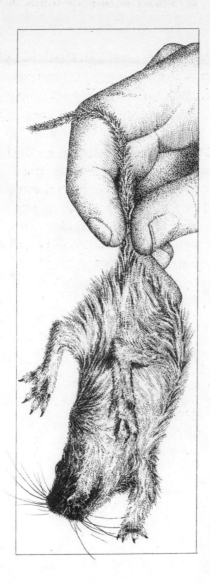

Live Baiting

It isn't nice, the way I fish:
Kidnapping roach from quiet ponds,
And spitting them on hooks
For pike to eat.
They swim, you could say, freely; live bait,
Unconstrained by locks,
But tethered by lip or fin, their bonds
Almost invisible, the barbs buried in flesh.

Each cast gives them the chance
To die. Scalded by air
They plummet thirty yards upstream,
Bombing the shallows, targets
That swim into the sights
Of what will kill them.
Pike aren't interested in playing at war,
They meet their partners in an older dance.

The one I caught today wore
Like a brooch a hook of mine, lost
When the line broke months ago.
I found it rooted
In her throat. When I gutted
Her, eggs lined her belly like orange sago.
Pain has no memory, grief stays in the past.
It isn't true. I can't fish this way any more.

Philip Oakes

We'll all be a-doubling, a-doubling.
We'll all be a-doubling in thirty-two years.

Pete Seeger

from *Slough*

Come, friendly bombs, and fall on Slough
It isn't fit for humans now,
There isn't grass to graze a cow
    Swarm over, Death!

Come, bombs, and blow to smithereens
Those air-conditioned, bright canteens,
Tinned fruit, tinned meat, tinned milk, tinned beans
    Tinned minds, tinned breath.

John Betjeman (1906–84)

77

Big Yellow Taxi

They paved paradise
And put up a parking lot
With a pink hotel, a boutique
And a swinging hot spot
Don't it always seem to go
That you don't know what you've got
Till it's gone
They paved paradise
And put up a parking lot.

They took all the trees
And put them in a tree museum
And they charged all the people
A dollar and a half just to see 'em
Don't it always seem to go
That you don't know what you've got
Till it's gone
They paved paradise
And put up a parking lot.

Hey farmer farmer
Put away that DDT now
Give me spots on my apples
But leave me the birds and the bees
Please!
Don't it always seem to go
That you don't know what you've got
Till it's gone
They paved paradise
And put up a parking lot.

Late last night
I heard the screen door slam
And a big yellow taxi
Took away my old man
Don't it always seem to go
That you don't know what you've got
Till it's gone
They paved paradise
And put up a parking lot.

Joni Mitchell

Telephone Poles

They have been with us a long time.
They will outlast the elms.
Our eyes, like the eyes of a savage sieving the trees
In his search for game,
Run through them. They blend along small-town streets
Like a race of giants that have faded into mere mythology.
Our eyes, washed clean of belief,
Lift incredulous to their fearsome crowns of bolts, trusses,
   struts, nuts, insulators, and such
Barnacles as compose
These weathered encrustations of electrical debris –
Each a Gorgon's head, which, seized right,
Could stun us to stone.

Yet they are ours. We made them.
See here, where the cleats of linemen
Have roughened a second bark
Onto the bald trunk. And these spikes
Have been driven sideways at intervals handy for human legs.
The Nature of our construction is in every way
A better fit than the Nature it displaces.
What other tree can you climb where the birds' twitter,
Unscrambled, is English? True, their thin shade is negligible,
But then again there is not that tragic autumnal
Casting-off of leaves to outface annually.
These giants are more constant than evergreens
By being never green.

John Updike

'Chill, burning rain'

Chill, burning rain
Has flayed the trees
And even evergreen
Will never green
To leaf again

John Kitching

Toothache Man

The earth has been unkind to him.
   He lies in middle strata.
The time capsules about him brim
   With advertising matter.

His addled fossils tell a tale
   That lacks barbaric splendor;
His vertebrae are small and pale,
   His femora are slender.

It is his teeth – strange, cratered things –
   That name him. Some are hollow,
Like bowls, and hold gold offerings.
   The god may be Apollo.

Silver and gold. We think he thought
   His god, who was immortal,
   Dwelt in his skull; hence, the devout
   Adorned the temple's portal.

Heraldic fists and spears and bells
   In all metallic colors
Invade the bone; their volume swells
   On backward through the molars.

This culture's meagre sediments
   Have come to light just lately.
We handle them with reverence.
   He must have suffered greatly.

                    John Updike

'Mummy, Oh Mummy'

'Mummy, Oh Mummy, what's this pollution
That everyone's talking about?'
'Pollution's the mess that the country is in,
That we'd all be far better without.
It's factories belching their fumes in the air,
And the beaches all covered with tar,
Now throw all those sweet papers into the bushes
Before we get back in the car.'

'Mummy, Oh Mummy, who makes pollution,
And why don't they stop if it's bad?'
''Cos people like that just don't think about others,
They don't think at all, I might add.
They spray all the crops and they poison the flowers,
And wipe out the birds and the bees,
Now there's a good place we could dump that old mattress
Right out of sight in the trees.'

'Mummy, Oh Mummy, what's going to happen
If all the pollution goes on?'
'Well the world will end up like a second-hand junk-yard,
With all of its treasures quite gone.
The fields will be littered with plastics and tins,
The streams will be covered with foam,
Now throw those two pop bottles over the hedge,
Save us from carting them home.'

'But Mummy, Oh Mummy, if I throw the bottles,
Won't that be polluting the wood?'
'Nonsense! that isn't the same thing at all,
You just shut up and be good.
If you're going to start getting silly ideas
I'm taking you home right away,
'Cos pollution is something that other folk do,
We're just enjoying our day.'

Anon

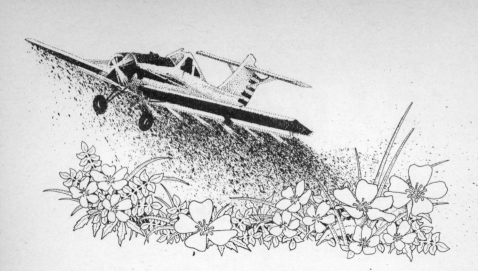

Harvest Hymn

We plough the fields and scatter
our pesticides again;
our seeds are fed and watered
by gentle acid rain.
We spray the corn in winter
till pests and weeds are dead –
who minds a little poison
inside his daily bread?

All good gifts around us
beneath our ozone layer
are safe, oh Lord,
so thank you Lord
that we know how to care.

Judith Nicholls

from *Benedicite, Omnia Opera*

O all ye Works of the Lord, bless ye the Lord:
praise him, and magnify him for ever . . .
   O ye Showers and Dew, bless ye the Lord:
praise him, and magnify him for ever.
   O ye Winds of God, bless ye the Lord:
praise him, and magnify him for ever.
   O ye Fire and Heat, bless ye the Lord:
praise him, and magnify him for ever.
   O ye Winter and Summer, bless ye the Lord:
praise him, and magnify him for ever.
   O ye Dews and Frosts, bless ye the Lord:
praise him, and magnify him for ever.
   O ye Frost and Cold, bless ye the Lord:
praise him, and magnify him for ever.
   O ye Ice and Snow, bless ye the Lord:
praise him, and magnify him for ever.
   O ye Nights and Days, bless ye the Lord:
praise him, and magnify him for ever.
   O ye Light and Darkness, bless ye the Lord:
praise him, and magnify him for ever.
   O ye Lightnings and Clouds, bless ye the Lord:
praise him, and magnify him for ever.
   O let the Earth bless the Lord: yea, let it
praise him, and magnify him for ever.
   O ye Mountains, and Hills, bless ye the Lord:
praise him, and magnify him for ever.
   O all ye Green Things upon the Earth, bless ye the
   Lord: praise him, and magnify him for ever.

Imagine that any mind ever *thought* a red geranium!
As if the redness of a red geranium could be anything but a
    sensual experience
and as if sensual experience could take place before there were
    any senses.
We know that even God could not imagine the redness of a red
    geranium
nor the smell of mignonette
when geraniums were not, and mignonette neither.
And even when they were, even God would have to have a
    nose
to smell at the mignonette.
You can't imagine the Holy Ghost sniffing at cherry-pie
    heliotrope.
Or the Most High, during the coal age, cudgelling his mighty
    brains
even if he had any brains: straining his mighty mind
to think, among the moss and mud of lizards and mastodons
to think out, in the abstract, when all was twilit green and
    muddy:
'Now there shall be tum-tiddly-um, and tum-tiddly-um,
hey-presto! scarlet geranium!'
We know it couldn't be done.

But imagine, among the mud and the mastodons
God sighing and yearning with tremendous creative yearning,
   in that dark green mess
oh, for some other beauty, some other beauty
that blossomed at last, red geranium, and mignonette.

D. H. Lawrence (1885–1930)

Where Have All the Flowers Gone?

Where have all the flowers gone,
Long time passing?
Where have all the flowers gone,
Long time ago?
Where have all the flowers gone?
The girls have picked them every one.
Oh, when will you ever learn?
Oh, when will you ever learn?

Where have all the young girls gone,
Long time passing?
Where have all the young girls gone,
Long time ago?
Where have all the young girls gone?
They've taken husbands every one.
Oh, when will you ever learn?
Oh, when will you ever learn?

Where have all the young men gone,
Long time passing?
Where have all the young men gone,
Long time ago?
Where have all the young men gone?
They're all in uniform.
Oh, when will we ever learn?
Oh, when will we ever learn?

Where have all the soldiers gone,
Long time passing?
Where have all the soldiers gone,
Long time ago?
Where have all the soldiers gone?
They've gone to graveyards, every one.
Oh, when will they ever learn?
Oh, when will they ever learn?

Where have all the graveyards gone,
Long time passing?
Where have all the graveyards gone,
Long time ago?
Where have all the graveyards gone?
They're covered with flowers every one.
Oh, when will they ever learn?
Oh, when will they ever learn?

Where have all the flowers gone,
Long time passing?
Where have all the flowers gone,
Long time ago?
Where have all the flowers gone?
Young girls picked them every one.
Oh, when will they ever learn?
Oh, when will they ever learn?

Pete Seeger

'They shall not wither'

They shall not wither, my flowers,
They shall not cease, my songs.
I, the singer, lift them up.
They are scattered, they spread about.
Even though on earth my flowers
may wither and yellow,
they will be carried there,
to the innermost house
of the bird with the golden feathers.

Anon, Aztec

Answer to a Question from the Emperor

I built roads

on hands and knees.
With mallet, chisel
we coaxed stone into shape
and with brown thumbs
gauged the spacing
for the carriage wheels.
We wasted none.

Our history is buried there.
A copper penny
beneath each thousandth stone.
A butterfly extinguished
by a calloused hand.
Seeds spilled from a serving wench,
cowslip in her hair,
drawn by the season
from the village
through the fields
in the deep heat
of a Friday afternoon.

Grass has smoothed
the gentle camber,
blanketed
the iron wheels.
Frost
does not dislocate
the stones.

And you, my lord?

John Latham

o sweet spontaneous
earth how often have
the
doting

      fingers of
prurient philosophers pinched
and
poked

thee
, has the naughty thumb
of science prodded
thy

   beauty .how
often have religions taken
thee upon their scraggy knees
squeezing and

buffeting thee that thou mightest conceive
gods
     (but
true

to the incomparable
couch of death thy
rhythmic
lover

    thou answerest

    them only with

           spring)

e.e. cummings (1894–1962)

Snake

A snake came to my water-trough
On a hot, hot day, and I in pyjamas for the heat,
To drink there.

In the deep, strange-scented shade of the great dark carob-tree
I came down the steps with my pitcher
And must wait, must stand and wait, for there he was at the
    trough before me.

He reached down from a fissure in the earth-wall in the gloom
And trailed his yellow-brown slackness soft-bellied down, over
    the edge of the stone trough
And rested his throat upon the stone bottom,
And where the water had dripped from the tap, in a small
    clearness,
He sipped with his straight mouth,
Softly drank through his straight gums, into his slack long
    body,
Silently.

Someone was before me at my water-trough,
And I, like a second comer, waiting.

He lifted his head from his drinking, as cattle do,
And looked at me vaguely, as drinking cattle do,
And flickered his two-forked tongue from his lips, and mused a
    moment,
And stooped and drank a little more,

Being earth-brown, earth-golden from the burning bowels of
   the earth
On the day of Sicilian July, with Etna smoking.

The voice of my education said to me
He must be killed,
For in Sicily the black, black snakes are innocent, the gold are
   venomous.

And voices in me said, If you were a man
You would take a stick and break him now, and finish him off.

But must I confess how I liked him,
How glad I was he had come like a guest in quiet, to drink at
   my water-trough
And depart peaceful, pacified, and thankless,
Into the burning bowels of this earth?

Was it cowardice, that I dared not kill him?
Was it perversity, that I longed to talk to him?
Was it humility, to feel so honoured?
I felt so honoured.

And yet those voices:
If you were not afraid, you would kill him!

And truly I was afraid, I was most afraid,
But even so, honoured still more
That he should seek my hospitality
From out the dark door of the secret earth.

He drank enough
And lifted his head, dreamily, as one who has drunken,
And flickered his tongue, like a forked night on the air, so
  black,
Seeming to lick his lips,
And looked around like a god, unseeing, into the air,
And slowly turned his head,
And slowly, very slowly, as if thrice adream,
Proceeded to draw his slow length curving round
And climb again the broken bank of my wall-face.

And as he put his head into that dreadful hole,
And as he slowly drew up, snake-easing his shoulders, and
  entered farther,
A sort of horror, a sort of protest against his withdrawing into
  that horrid black hole,
Deliberately going into the blackness, and slowly drawing
  himself after,
Overcame me now his back was turned.

I looked round, I put down my pitcher,
I picked up a clumsy log
And threw it at the water-trough with a clatter.

I think it did not hit him,
But suddenly that part of him that was left behind convulsed in
  undignified haste,
Writhed like lightning, and was gone
Into the black hole, the earth-lipped fissure in the wall-front,
At which, in the intense still noon, I stared with fascination.

And immediately I regretted it.
I thought how paltry, how vulgar, what a mean act!
I despised myself and the voices of my accursed human
   education.

And I thought of the albatross,
And I wished he would come back, my snake.

For he seemed to me again like a king,
Like a king in exile, uncrowned in the underworld,
Now due to be crowned again.

And so, I missed my chance with one of the lords
Of life.
And I have something to expiate;
A pettiness.

D. H. *Lawrence* (1885–1930)

Small Questions Asked by the Fat Black Woman

Will the rains
cleanse the earth of shrapnel
and wasted shells

will the seas
toss up bright fish
in wave on wave of toxic shoal

will the waters
seep the shore

feeding slowly the greying
angry roots

will trees bear fruit

will I like Eve
be tempted once again
if I survive

Grace Nichols

'There is joy'

There is joy in
Feeling the warmth
Come to the great world
And seeing the sun
Follow its old footprints
In the summer night.

There is fear in
Feeling the cold
Come to the great world
And seeing the moon
– Now new moon, now full moon –
Follow its old footprints
In the winter night.

Anon, Arctic Eskimo

'When the sun rises'

When the sun rises, I go to work,
When the sun goes down, I take my rest,
I dig the well from which I drink,
I farm the soil that yields my food,
I share creation, Kings can do no more.

Anon, Chinese (2500 BC)

Hoeing

I sometimes fear the younger generation will be deprived
   of the pleasures of hoeing;
   there is no knowing
how many souls have been formed by this simple exercise.

The dry earth like a great scab breaks, revealing
   moist-dark loam –
   the pea-root's home,
a fertile wound perpetually healing.

How neatly the green weeds go under!
   The blade chops the earth new.
   Ignorant the wise boy who
has never performed this simple, stupid, and useful wonder.

John Updike

Green Peace

All down the leafy country lane
The zummer zun's a-shinin'.
The 'edgerow wears a white lace cap
Wur elder bush be bloomin'.

Zweet little lambs is gambollin'
Along the ztreamzide bright,
Wur villains be a-stunnin' vish
Wi' zticks o' dynamite.

They likes ta poach our local brook,
Which tumbles o'er the weir
– Nobody's told 'em diesel vuel
Polluted it last year . . .

The bunny rabbits in the vields,
Wot's nibblin' varmer's carrots,
Will 'ave a shock wen they gets 'ome
– Their burrow's vull o' ferrets!

The 'orn-o'-plenty overflows
As 'arvest's yield increases,
While shootin' parties load their guns
An' blows the rooks ta pieces.

Ah . . . ! zummer-time's a 'appy time
vor zuch as 'ops or vlies
Or zwims about wi'out a care
– Zo long as they zurvives!

Keith Wilkins

Conservation Piece

The countryside must be preserved!
(Preferably miles away from me.)
Neat hectares of the stuff reserved
For those in need of flower or tree.

I'll make do with landscape painting
Film documentaries on TV.
And when I need to escape, panting,
Then open-mouthed I'll head for the sea.

Let others stroll and take their leisure,
In grasses wade up to their knees,
For I derive no earthly pleasure
From the green green rash that makes me sneeze.

Roger McGough

The earth does not belong to man;
man belongs to the earth.

Chief Seattle

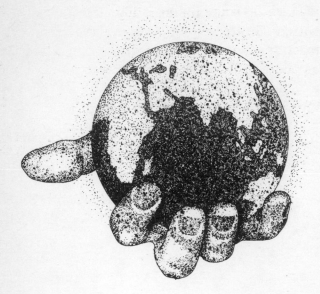

Prophecy

Eat, eat, thou hast bread;
Drink, drink, thou hast water;
On that day, dust possesses the earth,
On that day, a blight is on the face of the earth,
On that day, a cloud rises,
On that day, a mountain rises,
On that day, a strong man seizes the land,
On that day, things fall to ruin,
On that day, the tender leaf is destroyed,
On that day, the dying eyes are closed,
On that day, three signs are on the tree,
On that day, three generations hang there,
On that day, the battle flag is raised,
And they are scattered afar in the forests.

Anon, Mayan Indian

War Song

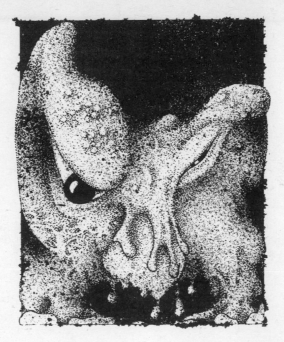

clear the way
in a sacred manner
I come
the earth
is mine

Anon, Sioux Indian

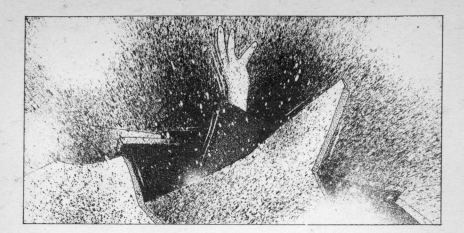

Fire and Ice

Some say the world will end in fire,
Some say in ice.
From what I've tasted of desire
I hold with those who favour fire.
But if it had to perish twice,
I think I know enough of hate
To say that for destruction ice
Is also great
And would suffice.

Robert Frost

1
The sun's beams are running out
The sun's beams are running out
The sun's yellow rays are running out
The sun's yellow rays are running out

2
We shall live again
We shall live again

Anon, Comanche Indian

'My flowers shall not perish'

My flowers shall not perish
Nor shall my chants cease
They spread, they scatter.

Anon, Aztec

Acknowledgements

For permission to reprint the poems in this anthology the editor and publishers gratefully acknowledge the following:

John Betjeman: 'Slough' (extract) from *Collected Poems* by John Betjeman, John Murray (Publishers) Ltd. Reprinted by permission of John Murray (Publishers) Ltd.

John Bierhorst: 'Prophecy', 'Songs of the Ghost Dance' and 'War Song' from *In the Trail of the Wind* by John Bierhorst. Copyright © 1971 by John Bierhorst. Reprinted by permission of Farrar, Straus and Giroux Inc.

Edwin Brock: 'Song of the Battery Hen' and '5 Ways to Kill a Man' reprinted by permission of David Higham Associates Ltd.

Alan Brownjohn: 'We are going to see the rabbit . . .' reprinted by permission of the author.

Hugh Chesterman: 'Noah and the Rabbit' reprinted by permission of Basil Blackwell Ltd.

William Cole: 'Back Yard, July Night' from *A Boy Named Mary Jane* copyright © 1977 William Cole. Reprinted by permission of the author.

e.e. cummings: 'o sweet spontaneous earth' from *Complete Poems 1913–1962*, Grafton Books, a division of the Collins Publishing Group. Reprinted by permission of Grafton Books.

R. T. Davies: 'Smoke-blackened Smiths' modern English trans. from *Medieval English Lyrics* trans. by R. T. Davies, Faber and Faber. Reprinted by permission of Faber and Faber Ltd.

Emily Dickinson: 'I robbed the Woods' and 'I lost a World' from *The Poems of Emily Dickinson* ed. by Thomas H. Johnson, Cambridge, Mass.: The Belknap Press of Harvard University Press, copyright © 1951, 1955, 1979, 1983 by the President and Fellows of Harvard College. Reprinted by permission of the publishers and the Trustees of Amherst College.

John. L. Foster: 'Graveyard Scene' by John L. Foster, © 1987, reprinted by permission of the author.

Robert Frost: 'Gathering Leaves' and 'Fire and Ice' from *The Poetry of Robert Frost* ed. by Edward Connery Lathem. Copyright © 1962 by Robert Frost. Copyright © 1975 by Lesley Frost Ballantine. Reprinted by permission of Jonathan Cape and Henry Holt and Company Inc.

111

Warner Bros Music Limited. Reprinted by permission of Warner Bros Music Limited.

Christian Morgenstern: 'The Hen' trans. by W. D. Snodgrass and Lore Segal, reprinted by permission of W. D. Snodgrass.

National Geographic Society: 'I Shall Vanish' Omaha Indian poem from the National Geographic Society Book Service's publication *The World of the American Indian*, © 1974, reprinted by permission of the National Geographic Society, Washington DC.

Judith Nicholls: 'Countdown', 'Harvest Festival' and 'Poem for the Rainforest' reprinted by permission of the author. 'Poem for the Rainforest' first appeared in *Midnight Forest* by Judith Nicholls, Faber and Faber.

Grace Nichols: 'Small questions asked by the fat black woman' from *Fat Black Woman's Poems* by Grace Nichols, copyright © Grace Nichols 1984. Reprinted by permission of Virago Press.

Norman Nicholson: 'Windscale' from *A Local Habitation* by Norman Nicholson, Faber and Faber. Reprinted by permission of David Higham Associates Limited.

Philip Oakes: 'Live Baiting' from *Selected Poems* by Philip Oakes (1982). Reprinted by permission of André Deutsch.

David Orme: 'The Day the Bulldozers Came' reprinted by permission of the author.

Tom Rawling: 'The Beck Insists' and 'Sap-Whistle' from *Ghosts at my Back* by Tom Rawling, Oxford University Press 1982, © Tom Rawling 1978, 1982. Reprinted by permission of Oxford University Press.

Theodore Roethke: 'Moss-gathering' from *The Collected Poems of Theodore Roethke* by Theodore Roethke, copyright © 1946 by Editorial Publications Inc. Reprinted by permission of Faber and Faber and of Doubleday, a division of Bantam Doubleday, Dell Publishing Group Inc.

Pete Seeger: 'Where have all the flowers gone?' © 1961 Harmony Music Ltd., 19/20 Poland Street, London W1V 3DD. International Copyright Secured. All Rights Reserved. Used by Permission.

Louisa-Jane Snook: 'The Last Human' reprinted by permission of the author.

Adam Stanley: 'Tree' from *Cadbury's Fourth Book of Children's Poetry*. Reproduced by permission of Cadbury Ltd.

John Updike: 'Sonic Boom', 'Telephone Poles', 'Toothache Man' and 'Hoeing' from *Telephone Poles and other Poems* by John Updike (1964) reprinted by permission of André Deutsch.

Keith Wilkins: 'Green Peace' from *Yer Tiz!* written and published by the author. Reprinted by permission of the author.

Raymond Wilson: 'Old Johnny Armstrong', 'This letter's to say' and 'Poisoned Talk' reprinted by permission of the author.

Adrian Youd: 'Felling Trees' reprinted by permission of the author.

Faber and Faber apologize for any errors or omissions in the above list and would be grateful to be notified of any corrections that should be incorporated in any future reprints.

Index of Poets

Index of First Lines

It isn't nice, the way I fish 76
It's not nostalgia, I don't 27

'Mummy, Oh Mummy, what's this pollution 84
My aspens dear, whose airy cages quelled 43
My flowers shall not perish 109

'No land,' said Noah 15
Noise of hammers once I heard 13
Nothing is so beautiful as Spring 5

O all ye Works of the Lord, bless ye the Lord 87
O Lord, how manifold are thy works! 32
Old Johnny Armstrong's eighty or more 25
On shallow straw, in shadeless glass 74
o sweet spontaneous 94

Pleasant it looked 1
Pleasure it is 2

Smooth-skinned sap-flooded 59
Some say the world will end in fire 108
Spades take up leaves 45
Stop! I cried to them 21
Summer's pleasures they are gone like to visions every one 52
Swarte-smeked smethes, smatered with smoke 12
Sweet smiling village, loveliest of the lawn 51

The animals are excited 58
The Combe was ever dark, ancient and dark 61
The countryside must be preserved! 104
The day the bulldozers came 67
The earth does not belong to man 105
The earth has been unkind to him 82
The flower-fed buffaloes of the spring 66
The girl forces the gull's beak open with 63
The poplars are fell'd, farewell to the shade 20
The shark is killed for its fin 62
The sun's beams are running out 109
The toadstool towers infest the shore 50
The world is charged with the grandeur of God 33

117

There are many cumbersome ways to kill a man 30
There are no names on the gravestones now 68
There are, some people say, no riches in the bush 37
There is joy in 101
They have been with us a long time 80
They have stolen my land 40
They paved paradise 78
They shall not wither, my flowers 92
This darksome burn, horseback brown 39
This then is life 59
To loosen with all ten fingers held wide and limber 19
To see a World in a Grain of Sand 38

We are going to see the rabbit 55
We can't grumble about accommodation 22
We plough the fields and scatter 86
We'll all be a' doubling, a-doubling 77
What cuckoos we are 71
When I heard the learn'd astronomer 28
When the goodies are all gone 31
When the sun rises, I go to work 101
Where have all the flowers gone 90
Who builds? Who builds? Alas, ye poor 11
Who killed cock robin? 69
Will the rains 100

You can't make whales 72
You could slake a small thirst 44